Felt is fantastic for crafting kid's projects! Simply use the patterns and step-by-step instructions in this book to create seven play mats that boys and girls will love. Each goes together easily with a bit of glue and stitching.

LEISURE ARTS, INC. • Maumelle, Arkansas

Magical Castle

Finished Size: 12½" x 18"

SHOPPING LIST

- ☐ 1 sheet of light tan felt
- ☐ 1 sheet of white felt
- ☐ 1 sheet of pink felt
- ☐ 12" x 22" piece of hot pink felt
- ☐ 1 sheet of yellow felt
- ☐ 1 sheet of dark yellow felt
- ☐ 1 sheet of light green felt
- ☐ 13½" x 44" piece of green felt
- ☐ 3 2" tall wooden peg dolls

- ☐ 5 2³/₈" tall wooden trees
- ☐ various colors of acrylic paint
- ☐ paintbrushes
- ☐ wooden toothpicks
- ☐ hot pink and black 6-strand embroidery floss
- ☐ embroidery needle
- ☐ scissors
- ☐ low-temp glue gun and glue sticks
- ☐ tracing paper

*Please read **General Instructions**,
pages 46-47, before beginning project.*

Cutting

Note: *Use patterns on pages 36, 37, & 39.*

1. From light tan felt, freehand cut 30-35 assorted round- and oval-shaped rocks as desired.
2. From white felt, use pattern to cut 2 unicorns.
3. From pink felt, use pattern to cut 1 robe.
4. From hot pink felt, use patterns to cut 2 castle walls, 1 base, 2 unicorn manes, and 1 unicorn tail.
5. From yellow felt, use patterns to cut 1 unicorn horn, 1 crown, 1 robe clasp, and 15-20 small flowers.
6. From dark yellow, pink, hot pink, and white felt, use patterns to cut 18-25 assorted large and medium flowers as desired.
7. From green felt, cut 2 mats 12$\frac{1}{2}$" x 18". Use pattern to cut grass.
8. From light green and green felt, use patterns to cut 25-30 assorted leaves as desired.

To make the Magical Castle

Note: *Refer to **Embroidery Stitches**, page 47, for stitch techniques. Use 3 strands of floss for all stitching.*

Making the Castle

1. Stack and glue the castle walls together. Using hot pink floss and Whipstitches, stitch the doorway edges together. To stitch the castle walls to the base, begin on one side of the doorway and whipstitch the bottom edge to the base until you get near the back. Repeat to stitch the remaining side of the castle walls to the base. The back of the castle may overlap. Trim off any excess felt along the back edge. Whipstitch the back edges together.

Tip:
It's hard to stitch through areas where you have applied glue. When stacking and gluing pieces, make sure to leave the area where you will be stitching free of glue.

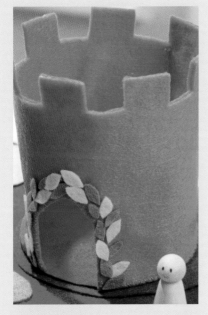

2. Add glue along the castle wall edges as needed to secure the layers together. Glue the leaves around the doorway as desired.

3. Glue the castle to the grass.

Making the Trees and People

4. Use desired paint colors to paint trees and peg dolls. Using a toothpick, add tiny mouths and eyes to the peg dolls.

5. For the princess, wrap the robe around 1 of the peg dolls and glue near the neck. Glue the robe clasp to the robe.

6. Glue the crown to the princess, trimming the ends of the crown as needed.

Making the Unicorn

7. Using black floss and Backstitches, stitch the unicorn's mouth on each piece. Using small Cross Stitches, stitch the unicorn's eye on each piece.

8. Leaving the legs free, sandwich the horn and tail between the layers and glue the unicorns together.

9. Glue 1 mane to each side of the unicorn.

Making the Mat

10. Stack the mats together and glue. Use scissors to round the corners.

11. Glue the rocks and flowers to the mat as desired to create a path.

Sea Life

Finished Size: 18" x 21"

SHOPPING LIST

- ☐ 8" x 27" piece of light tan felt
- ☐ 2 sheets of brown felt
- ☐ 1 sheet of black felt
- ☐ 1 sheet of hot pink felt
- ☐ 18" x 7" piece of light blue felt
- ☐ 22" x 37" piece of bright blue felt
- ☐ 1 sheet of green felt
- ☐ 1 sheet of bright green felt

- ☐ 1 sheet of yellow felt
- ☐ 1 sheet of dark yellow felt
- ☐ 1 sheet of orange felt
- ☐ black and brown 6-strand embroidery floss
- ☐ embroidery needle
- ☐ scissors
- ☐ low-temp glue gun and glue sticks
- ☐ tracing paper

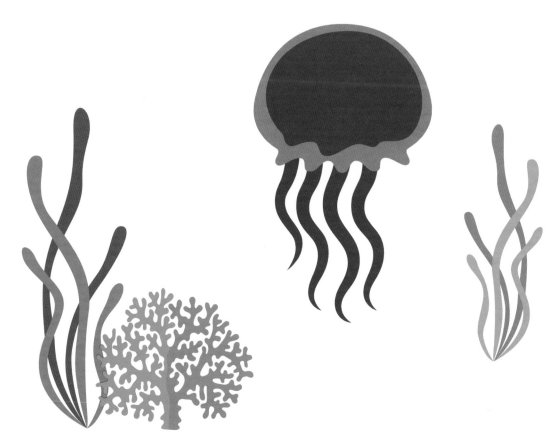

To make our underwater world come to life even more, we added small plastic aquatic animals.

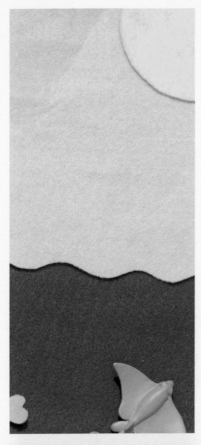

*Please read **General Instructions**, pages 46-47, before beginning project.*

Cutting

Note: *Use patterns on pages 42-45.*

1. From light tan felt, cut 1 rectangle 6^1/$_2$" x 18". Use scissors to trim 1 long edge randomly for ocean floor. Use pattern to cut beach.
2. From brown felt, use patterns to cut 2 ships and 2 masts.
3. From black felt, use pattern to cut 2 portholes.
4. From hot pink felt, cut 2 sea anemones 1" x 4".
5. From light blue felt, use scissors to trim 1 long edge randomly for sky.
6. From bright blue felt, cut 2 mats 18" x 21".
7. From green felt, use pattern to cut seaweed.
8. From bright green and dark yellow felt, use patterns to cut desired number of large and small fish (each fish requires 2 pieces).
9. From yellow felt, cut 2 sea anemones 1" x 4". Use pattern to cut sun.
10. From orange felt, cut 1 sea anemone 1" x 4". Use pattern to cut 1 coral.

To make the Seascape

Note: *Refer to **Embroidery Stitches**, page 47, for stitch techniques.*

Making the Ship

1. To make the ship, use 6 strands of brown floss and Backstitches to stitch horizontal lines on 1 ship to create the wood grain.

2. With the stitched ship on top, glue the ships together.

3. Glue the masts together. Glue the mast to the back of the ship.

4. Glue the portholes to the ship.

Making the Fish

5. To make a fish, use 2 strands of black floss and small Straight Stitches to make an eye on 2 fish. Glue 2 fish together. Make as many fish as desired.

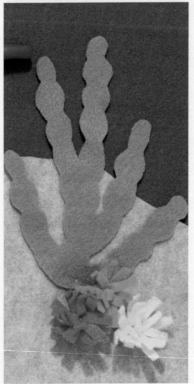

Making the Mat

6. Stack and glue the mats together.

7. Glue the sky, ocean floor, beach, and sun to the mat.

8. Glue the ship, coral, and seaweed to the mat.

9. To create a sea anemone, cut $3/4$" deep slits about $1/4$" apart along 1 long edge. Add a drop of glue near 1 end. Adding glue as you go, roll it up. Make a total of 5 sea anemone. Glue each sea anemone to the mat.

Sweet Cupcake Shop

Finished Size: 11¹/₂" x 18"

SHOPPING LIST

- ☐ 12¹/₂" x 2¹/₂" piece of light tan felt
- ☐ 1 sheet of tan felt
- ☐ 2 sheets of cream felt
- ☐ 1 sheet of brown felt
- ☐ 1 sheet of black felt
- ☐ 1 sheet of gray felt
- ☐ 1 sheet of white felt
- ☐ 2 sheets of blue felt
- ☐ 12¹/₂" x 45" piece of light pink felt
- ☐ 1 sheet of pink felt
- ☐ 1 sheet of hot pink felt
- ☐ 1 sheet of red felt
- ☐ 1 sheet of light yellow felt
- ☐ 18" of ¹/₈" wide light pink ribbon
- ☐ brown, gray, black, turquoise, red, light pink, pink, hot pink, light green, and yellow 6-strand embroidery floss
- ☐ embroidery needle
- ☐ scissors
- ☐ low-temp glue gun and glue sticks
- ☐ tracing paper

Tip:
It's hard to stitch through areas where you have applied glue. When stacking and gluing pieces, make sure to leave the area where you will be stitching free of glue.

*Please read **General Instructions**, pages 46-47, before beginning project.*

Cutting

Note: *Use patterns on pages 34-36.*

1. From light tan felt, cut 1 bottom strip $3/4$" x $11^1/2$" and 1 middle strip $5/8$" x $11^1/2$". Use scissors to round corners slightly.

2. From cream felt, cut display case $4^5/8$" x 8", 3 shelves $1/8$" x $4^5/8$", 1 bowl stripe $1/8$" x $2^7/8$" and 1 bowl stripe $3/8$" x $2^7/8$". Use patterns to cut display case scallop, cake stand with scallop, and cake stand scallop only.

3. From brown felt, use pattern to cut 1 small cupcake.

4. From black felt, cut 1 oven handle $1/8$" x 2" and 1 oven handle $1/8$" x $3/4$". Use patterns to cut 1 large knob and 4 small knobs.

5. From gray felt, use patterns to cut 2 spoons and 2 ovens. For oven door, cut window opening from 1 oven along gray line.

6. From white felt, use pattern to cut 1 large cupcake.

7. From blue felt, cut 1 cupcake pocket 2" x 9" and 3 strips $1/4$" x 2". Use patterns to cut 1 bowl and 1 circle.

8. From light pink felt, cut 2 cases $11^1/2$" x 18". Use pattern to cut 4 handles.

9. From pink felt, use patterns to cut 1 large frosting and 1 small frosting.

10. From hot pink felt, use patterns to cut 1 large scallop.

11. From red felt, cut 1 large cherry, 12 medium cherries, and 1 small cherry.

12. From tan, brown, and pink felt, use pattern to cut a total of 12 medium cupcakes in desired colors.

13. From light yellow, brown, pink, and hot pink felt, use pattern to cut a total of 12 matching pairs of medium frostings.

To make the Cupcake Shop

Note: *Refer to* **Embroidery Stitches**, *page 47, for stitch techniques. Use 3 strands of embroidery floss unless otherwise indicated.*

Making the Outer Case

1. Stack and glue 2 handles together. Using 6 strands of light pink floss and Running Stitches, stitch along the handle edges. Repeat to make a second handle.

2. Cut the ribbon in half. Tie a knot near 1 end of each piece.

3. Sandwiching 1 handle and 1 knotted ribbon end between the layers at the center of each short edge, stack and glue the cases together. The knot helps keep the ribbon in place. Using light pink floss and Running Stitches, stitch along the long edges of the case.

4. Using 6 strands of desired colors of floss and Straight Stitches, stitch sprinkles on the large frosting as desired. Use 6 strands of red floss and small Straight Stitches to stitch the large cherry to the large frosting.

5. To decorate the case front, glue the large scallop, circle, large cupcake, and large frosting to the case.

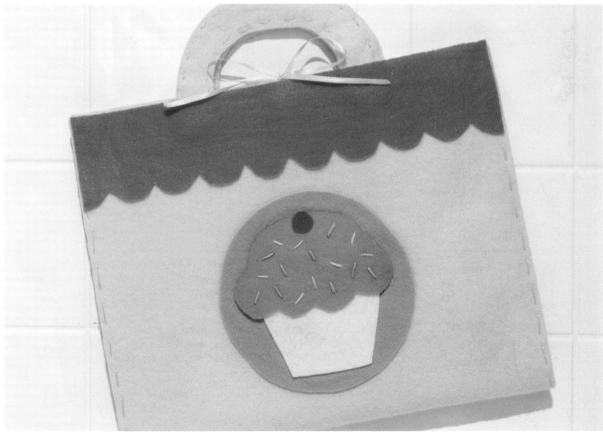

Making the Inside Case

6. Glue the bottom strip to the inside of the case on the same end as the large scallop. Fold the case in half to find the center fold. Glue the middle strip just above the fold line.

7. Glue the display case, display case scallop, and shelves just above the bottom strip.

8. Glue the cake stand just above the bottom strip. Glue the cake stand scallop to the cake stand.

9. Center the cupcake pocket 1" from the top of the case; glue along the side and bottom edges. To divide into 2 pockets, glue the pocket to the case in the center. Glue the blue strips along each end and in the center of the pocket. Using 2 strands of desired colors of floss and Straight Stitches, stitch sprinkles on the small frosting as desired. Glue the small cherry to the small frosting. Glue the small cupcake and small frosting to the pocket.

10. Glue the stripes to the bowl. Glue the bowl to the case along the curved edge.

11. Stack the spoons. Using gray floss and Backstitches, stitch the spoons together around the edges.

12. To make the oven door, use gray floss and Backstitches to stitch around the oven window opening. Using gray floss and Running Stitches, stitch around the outer edge of the oven door. Glue the knobs to the oven door. Using 6 strands of black floss and Backstitches, stitch a line below the knobs and about 1^1/$_4$" above the bottom edge of the door. Glue the handles to the oven door.

13. The oven door opens and closes. Stack the two oven pieces together and glue from the bottom backstitched line to the bottom of the door. Glue the oven to the case.

Making the Cupcakes

14. Using desired colors of floss and Straight Stitches, stitch sprinkles on half of the medium frostings as desired.

15. Glue a medium cherry to each embroidered medium frosting.

16. Stack 1 embroidered frosting piece on top of 1 matching plain frosting piece. Using matching floss and Running Stitches, stitch frosting pieces together along the top and sides. Leave the bottom open so it can slide over the medium cupcake. Make 12 frostings.

Campsite

Finished Size: 18" x 24"

SHOPPING LIST

- ☐ 1 sheet of light tan felt
- ☐ 1 sheet of brown felt
- ☐ 1 sheet of blue felt
- ☐ 1 sheet of aqua felt
- ☐ 1 sheet of yellow felt
- ☐ 1 sheet of dark yellow felt
- ☐ 1 sheet of pink felt
- ☐ 1 sheet of hot pink felt
- ☐ 3 sheets of red felt
- ☐ 1 sheet of moss green felt
- ☐ 1 sheet of bright green felt
- ☐ 19" x 49" piece of green felt

- ☐ 2 1³/₄" tall wooden peg dolls
- ☐ 1 1¹/₄" tall wooden peg doll
- ☐ 3 2³/₈" tall wooden trees
- ☐ various colors of acrylic paint
- ☐ paintbrushes
- ☐ wooden toothpicks
- ☐ aqua, dark yellow, red, and green 6-strand embroidery floss
- ☐ embroidery needle
- ☐ scissors
- ☐ low-temp glue gun and glue sticks
- ☐ tracing paper

*Please read **General Instructions**,*
pages 46-47, before beginning project.

Cutting

Note: Use patterns on pages 37-38, 40-42, & 45.

1. From light tan felt, use pattern to cut dirt.
2. From brown felt, use patterns to cut mud and 12-15 logs.
3. From blue felt, use pattern to cut pond.
4. From aqua felt, cut large sleeping bag 2" x 5".
5. From yellow felt, use patterns to cut medium flame and desired large flowers.
6. From dark yellow felt, use pattern to cut large flame. Cut small sleeping bag $1^5/8$" x $3^1/4$".
7. From pink felt, use pattern to cut desired large flowers.
8. From hot pink felt, use pattern to cut desired large flowers.
9. From red felt, cut tent sides 9" x 10" and tent bottom 5" x $8^1/2$". Use pattern to cut tent back, small flame, boat bottom, boat back, small boat seat, large boat seat, and 2 boat sides.
10. From moss green felt, use pattern to cut 3 pieces of grass.
11. From bright green felt, cut large sleeping bag 2" x 5".
12. From green felt, cut 2 mats 18" x 24".

To make the Campsite

*Note: Refer to **Embroidery Stitches**, page 47, for stitch techniques.*

Making the Tent

Use 6 strands of red floss and Whipstitches when assembling the tent.

1. Fold the tent sides in half to measure 5" x 9"; glue the long edges together. Matching short ends, fold in half again; **do not** glue. Stitch along the fold to make the tent peak.

2. Matching short ends, fold tent bottom in half to measure $4^1/4$" x 5"; glue layers together. Stitch the tent sides to the tent bottom.

3. With the folded edge of the tent sides in front, glue the tent back to the back along the sides and bottom.

Making the Campfire

4. Stack and glue the bottom edge of each flame together.

5. Glue the bottom edge of the flames to 1 log. Stack and glue desired number of logs around the flames.

Making the Boat

Use 3 strands of red floss and Whipstitches when assembling the boat.

6. Stitch the boat sides together at the short end.

7. Stitch boat sides to short ends of the boat back.

8. Stitch the sides and back to the boat bottom.

9. To attach the seats, glue the end of each seat to the bottom of the boat sides. The seats will puff up a bit.

Making the Sleeping Bags

Use 3 strands of coordinating floss and Running Stitches when assembling the sleeping bags.

10. Stitch along 1 short end of 1 large sleeping bag.

11. Fold stitched end over 2". Stitch around outside edge of sleeping bag.

12. Repeat Steps 10-11 to make another large sleeping bag and 1 small sleeping bag, folding small sleeping bag over 1¹⁄₄".

Making the Mat

13. Stack and glue the mats together.

14. Glue the pond, dirt, mud, and large flowers to the mat as desired.

15. To make 1 piece of grass, accordion fold the grass, adding glue as you go. Make a total of 3 grass pieces. Glue them around the pond.

16. Use desired paint colors to paint trees and people. Using a toothpick, add tiny mouths, eyes, and dots on dress.

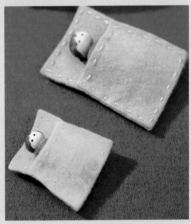

Down Home Farm

Finished Size: 18" x 19"

SHOPPING LIST

- [ ] 19" x 39" piece of green felt
- [ ] 1 sheet of bright green felt
- [ ] 1 sheet of light green felt
- [ ] 1 sheet of moss green felt
- [ ] 1 sheet of blue felt
- [ ] 1 sheet of yellow felt
- [ ] 1 sheet of orange felt
- [ ] 1 sheet of brown felt
- [ ] 1 sheet of tan felt
- [ ] 1 sheet of light tan felt
- [ ] 2 sheets of white felt
- [ ] 1 large sheet (12" x 18") of red stiffened felt
- [ ] 1 large sheet (12" x 18") of white stiffened felt
- [ ] red, light green, and green 6-strand embroidery floss
- [ ] embroidery needle
- [ ] scissors
- [ ] low-temp glue gun and glue sticks
- [ ] tracing paper

*Please read **General Instructions**, pages 46-47, before beginning project.*

Cutting

Note: *Use patterns on pages 38-41.*

1. From green felt, cut 2 mats 18" x 19".
2. From bright green felt, use patterns to cut 2 plants, 8 carrot tops, 6 small corn husks, and 12 large corn husks.
3. From light green felt, use pattern to cut 4 cabbages.
4. From moss green felt, use pattern to cut 2 plants.
5. From blue felt, use pattern to cut 1 pond.
6. From yellow felt, use patterns to cut loft window and 6 ears of corn.
7. From orange felt, use pattern to cut 3 carrots.
8. From brown felt, cut the garden base 4" x 5^1/$_2$". Use scissors to round the corners.
9. From tan felt, cut 2 floor pieces 5^1/$_2$" x 6", 5 garden rows ^{1}/$_2$" x 3^1/$_2$", desired number of hay strips ^{1}/$_8$" x 1^1/$_2$", and 2 hay binding strips ^{1}/$_8$" x 2^1/$_2$" for each desired hay bale. Use pattern to cut desired number of hay stack bases.
10. From light tan felt, freehand cut 12-17 rocks.
11. From white felt, cut 5 narrow fence rails ^{1}/$_4$" x 9" and 10 wide fence rails ^{1}/$_2$" x 9". Use pattern to cut 40 fence posts.
12. From red stiffened felt, cut 2 barn sides 5" x 4". Use pattern to cut 1 barn front and 1 barn back. Cut door from barn front on gray lines.
13. From white stiffened felt, cut roof 5^1/$_4$" x 10".

Tip:
It's hard to stitch through areas where you have applied glue. When stacking and gluing pieces, make sure to leave the area where you will be stitching free of glue.

To make the Farmyard

Note: *Refer to* **Embroidery Stitches**, *page 47, for stitch techniques.*

Making the Barn

1. Stitching from bottom to top, use 3 strands of red floss and Whipstitches to stitch the barn front, sides, and back together.

2. Stack and glue the floor pieces together.

3. Center the barn walls on the floor and Whipstitch in place.

4. Matching short ends, fold roof in half; crease. This will be the peak of the roof. Glue the roof to the barn walls.

5. Glue the loft window to the barn front.

Making the Fences

6. To make 1 fence section, lay down 1 wide fence rail with 1 narrow fence rail above it. Evenly space 8 fence posts along the rails. Glue the fence posts to the rails. Glue 1 wide fence rail on top of the other wide fence rail with the fence posts sandwiched in between.

7. Repeat Step 6 to make 5 fence sections.

8. Overlapping ends, glue 3 fence sections together to make 1 fence. Glue remaining sections together to make another fence.

Making the Garden

9. Glue the garden rows to the garden base.

10. To make the corn plants, glue 2 large corn husks, 1 small corn husk, and 1 ear of corn together. Make 6 corn plants. Glue corn plants to 2 garden rows.

14. To make a hay bale, stack and glue desired number of hay strips together; glue 2 hay binding strips around group. Make desired number of hay bales.

15. To make a hay stack, stack and glue desired number of hay strips on top of 1 hay stack base. Make desired number of hay stacks.

11. To make the carrots, glue 1 carrot top around 1 carrot. Make a total of 3 carrots. Glue carrots to garden rows.

12. To make the remaining carrot tops, add a drop of glue near the bottom edge of 1 carrot top; roll it up. Make a total of 5 carrot tops. Glue carrot tops to garden rows.

13. To make the cabbages, use 2 strands of floss and a Running Stitch to stitch around the outer edge of the cabbage. Pull the floss tight; knot. Make a total of 4 cabbages. Glue cabbages to a garden row.

Making the Mat

16. Stack and glue the mats together. Using 6 strands of green floss and Running Stitches, stitch along the edges.

17. Glue the pond to the mat; glue rocks around the pond as desired.

18. To create a plant, add a drop of glue near 1 end of 1 moss green plant. Adding glue as you go, roll it up. Add a drop of glue near 1 end of 1 bright green plant. Adding glue as you go, roll it around the moss green plant. Make a total of 2 plants. Glue the plants around the pond as desired.

27

Woodland Wonderland

Finished Size: 12" x 9"

SHOPPING LIST

- ☐ 13" x 25" piece of green felt
- ☐ 2 sheets of bright green felt
- ☐ 1 sheet of blue felt
- ☐ 1 sheet of light blue felt
- ☐ 1 sheet of red felt
- ☐ 1 sheet of pink felt
- ☐ 1 sheet of light pink felt
- ☐ 1 sheet of brown felt
- ☐ 1 sheet of tan felt
- ☐ 1 sheet of light tan felt
- ☐ 1 sheet of dark gray felt
- ☐ 1 sheet of cream felt
- ☐ 1 sheet of white felt
- ☐ 3 $1^3/_4$" tall wooden peg dolls
- ☐ red, pink, brown, and black 6-strand embroidery floss
- ☐ embroidery needle
- ☐ scissors
- ☐ low-temp glue gun and glue sticks
- ☐ tracing paper

*Please read **General Instructions**, pages 46-47, before beginning project.*

Cutting

Note: *Use patterns on pages 38-39, 41, and 43-45.*

1. From green felt, cut 2 mats 12" x 9". Use pattern to cut 2 cottage bottoms.
2. From bright green felt, cut 6 trees and 8 leaves.
3. From blue felt, use pattern to cut river.
4. From light blue felt, cut 2 windows $1^1/_8$" x $1^1/_8$".
5. From red felt, use pattern to cut 1 roof.
6. From pink felt, use patterns to cut 4 tulips and desired number of pansies.
7. From light pink felt, use patterns to cut desired number of pansies.
8. From brown felt, cut 2 window boxes $^1/_8$" x $1^1/_8$". Use patterns to cut 2 doors, 2 hedgehog spines, and 2 hedgehog noses.
9. From tan felt, use patterns to cut 2 hedgehog bodies and 2 squirrels.
10. From light tan felt, cut 1 door knob, and a total of 7-10 small and large stepping stones.
11. From dark gray felt, use pattern to cut 2 rabbits.
12. From cream felt, use pattern to cut 2 rabbits.
13. From white felt, cut 2 walls $2^1/_2$" x 9". Use patterns to cut 5-7 assorted dots.

To make the Woodland Wonderland

Note: *Refer to **Embroidery Stitches**, page 47, for stitch techniques. Use 3 strands of floss unless otherwise indicated.*

Making the Animals

1. To make the squirrel, use 2 strands of black floss and a Straight Stitch to stitch the squirrel's mouth on each piece. Using small Straight Stitches, stitch the squirrel's eye on each piece.

2. Leaving the legs free, glue the squirrels together.

3. To make each rabbit, use pink floss and small Straight Stitches to stitch the rabbit's eye on each piece.

12. With the stitched door on top, glue the doors together. Using brown floss and Whipstitches, stitch the door to the side of the opening.

13. Using brown floss and Backstitches, stitch the window frame and window panes on each window. Glue the windows to the cottage. Glue the window box to the bottom of the window. Glue tulips and leaves to each window box.

4. Leaving the legs free, glue the rabbits together. Make 1 cream rabbit and 1 dark gray rabbit.

5. To make the hedgehog, use brown floss and small Straight Stitches to stitch the hedgehog's eye on each hedgehog body.

6. Leaving the legs free, glue the hedgehog bodies together.

7. Glue the hedgehog spines to each side of the hedgehog body. Glue a nose to each side of the hedgehog.

Making the Cottage

8. Stack and glue the walls together. Fold walls in half to find the center. Matching centers, place 1 door on walls. For opening, cut along edge of door. Overlapping slightly, glue the short ends of the walls together.

9. Stack and glue the cottage bottoms together. Glue the walls to the cottage bottom.

10. Using red floss and Whipstitches, stitch straight edges of roof together. Glue dots to roof. Glue the roof to the walls.

11. To make the door, use brown floss and Backstitches to stitch the wood grain pattern on 1 door. Using brown floss and Straight Stitches, stitch the door knob to the door.

Making the Trees

14. Leaving the bottom open, stack and glue 2 trees together along the outer edges.

15. Glue wooden peg doll inside the tree.

16. Repeat Steps 14-15 to make a total of 3 trees.

Making the Mat

17. Stack and glue the mats together. Use scissors to round the corners.

18. Glue the river to the mat as desired.

19. Glue the stepping stones to the mat as desired to create a path.

20. Glue assorted-color pansies to the mat.

On The Road

Finished Size: 14" x 18½"

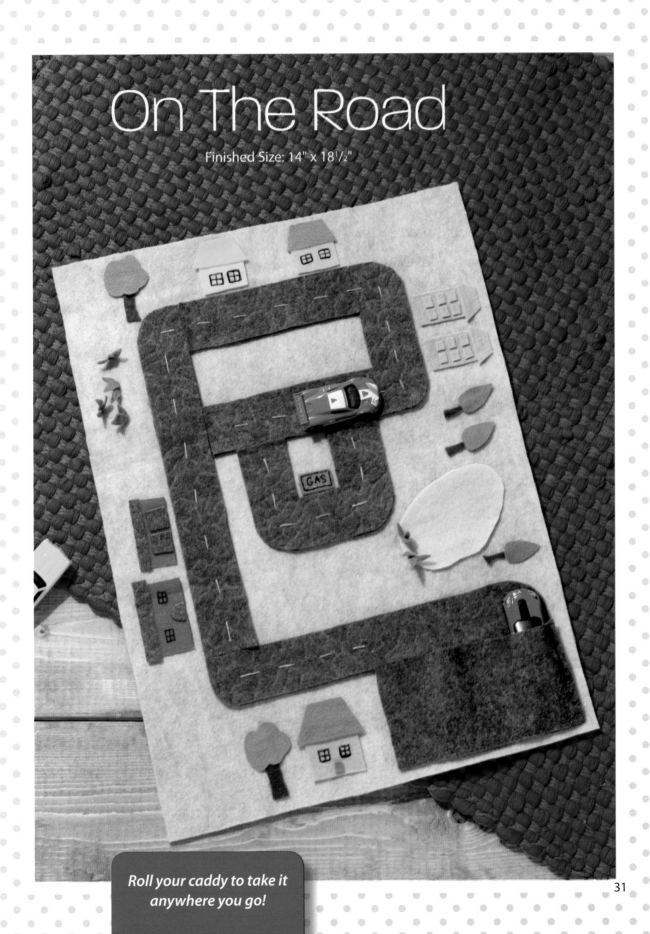

Roll your caddy to take it anywhere you go!

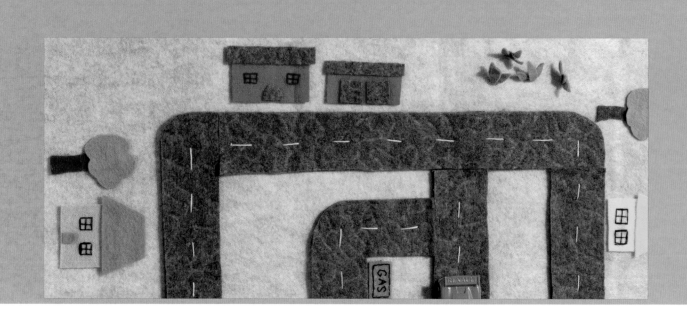

SHOPPING LIST

- [ ] 15" x 38" piece of light tan felt
- [ ] 1 sheet of light gray felt
- [ ] 3 sheets of dark gray felt
- [ ] 1 sheet of light blue felt
- [ ] 1 sheet of blue felt
- [ ] 1 sheet of aqua felt
- [ ] 1 sheet of red felt
- [ ] 1 sheet of yellow felt
- [ ] 1 sheet of dark yellow felt
- [ ] 1 sheet of light green felt
- [ ] 1 sheet of dark green felt
- [ ] 1 sheet of moss green felt
- [ ] 1 sheet of brown felt
- [ ] yellow and black 6-strand embroidery floss
- [ ] embroidery needle
- [ ] scissors
- [ ] low-temp glue gun and glue sticks
- [ ] tracing paper

*Please read **General Instructions**, pages 46-47, before beginning project.*

Cutting

Note: *Use patterns on pages 39 & 41-43.*

1. From light tan felt, cut 2 mats 14" x $18^1/_2$".
2. From light gray felt, cut 1 house $1^3/_4$" x $1^1/_2$" and 12 windows $3/_8$" x $1/_4$". Use pattern to cut 2 small roofs.
3. From dark gray felt, use patterns to cut 2 roads and 1 large door. Also cut:
   - 2 large garages $6^1/_4$" x $3^1/_2$"
   - 4 roads $1^5/_8$" x 11"
   - 4 roads $1^5/_8$" x $5^3/_4$"
   - 2 roads $1^5/_8$" x 5"
   - 1 large roof $1/_2$" x $2^1/_2$".
   - 1 small roof $3/_8$" x $2^1/_4$".
   - 2 garage doors $5/_8$" x $5/_8$".
4. From light blue felt, use pattern to cut 1 pond.
5. From blue felt, use patterns to cut 1 large roof and 1 small door. Cut 1 gas sign $5/_8$" x $1^1/_8$".
6. From aqua felt, cut 2 office buildings 1" x $1^3/_4$".
7. From red felt, cut 1 house $1^1/_4$" x $2^1/_4$" and 1 garage 1" x $2^1/_8$".
8. From yellow felt, cut 1 house 1" x $1^1/_2$".
9. From dark yellow felt, use pattern to cut 1 medium roof.
10. From light green felt, cut 1 house 1" x $1^1/_2$".
11. From dark green felt, use pattern to cut 1 medium roof.
12. From moss green felt, use patterns to cut 2 oak tree tops, 3 maple tree tops, and 18 grasses.
13. From brown felt, use patterns to cut 2 oak tree trunks and 3 maple tree trunks.

To make the Caddy

*Note: Refer to **Embroidery Stitches**, page 47, for stitch techniques. Use 2 strands of floss unless otherwise indicated.*

Making the Caddy

1. Glue the large garages together along 1 long edge and 2 short edges. Glue 2 evenly spaced lines to create 3 car slots.

2. Glue 2 matching road pieces together along the outer edges. Repeat with all road pieces.

3. Using scissors to round road corners as needed, glue the road pieces and the large garage to 1 mat.

4. Use 3 strands of yellow floss and Running Stitches to stitch along the center of the road through all layers.

5. To make caddy, stack this mat on the remaining mat and glue the layers together.

Adding the Buildings

6. Use black floss and Backstitches to stitch the window frames on each house. Use black floss and Straight Stitches to stitch the window panes on each house.

7. Glue small door to gray house. Glue large door to red house. Glue gray garage doors to red garage. Glue light gray windows to aqua office buildings.

8. Glue houses, office buildings, garage, and roofs to caddy.

Completing the Caddy

9. Glue the pond, tree trunks, and tree tops to the caddy.

10. Use black floss and Backstitches to stitch the gas sign. Glue the sign to the caddy.

11. Glue the grass to the caddy and pond in groups of 3.

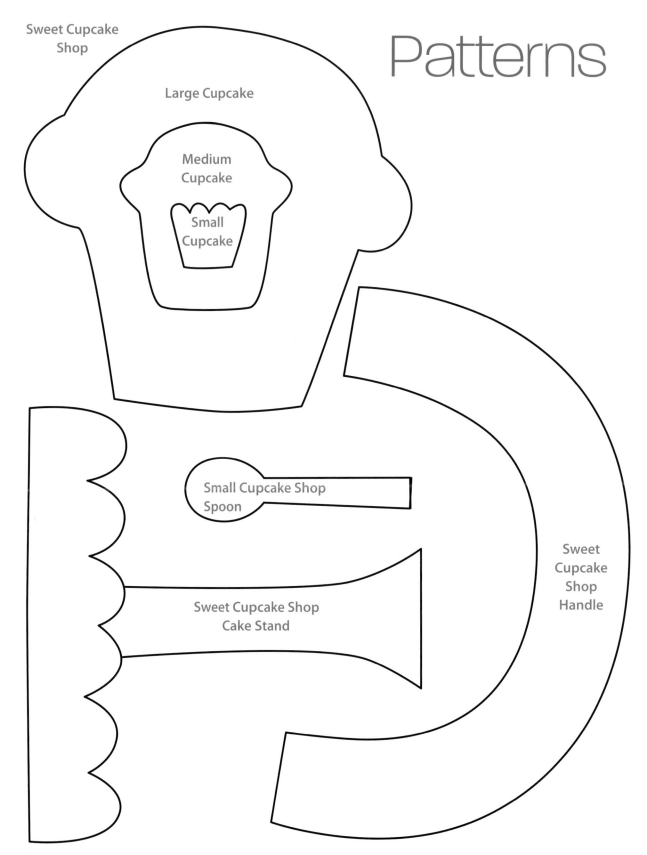

Sweet Cupcake Shop

Patterns

Large Cupcake

Medium Cupcake

Small Cupcake

Small Cupcake Shop Spoon

Sweet Cupcake Shop Handle

Sweet Cupcake Shop Cake Stand

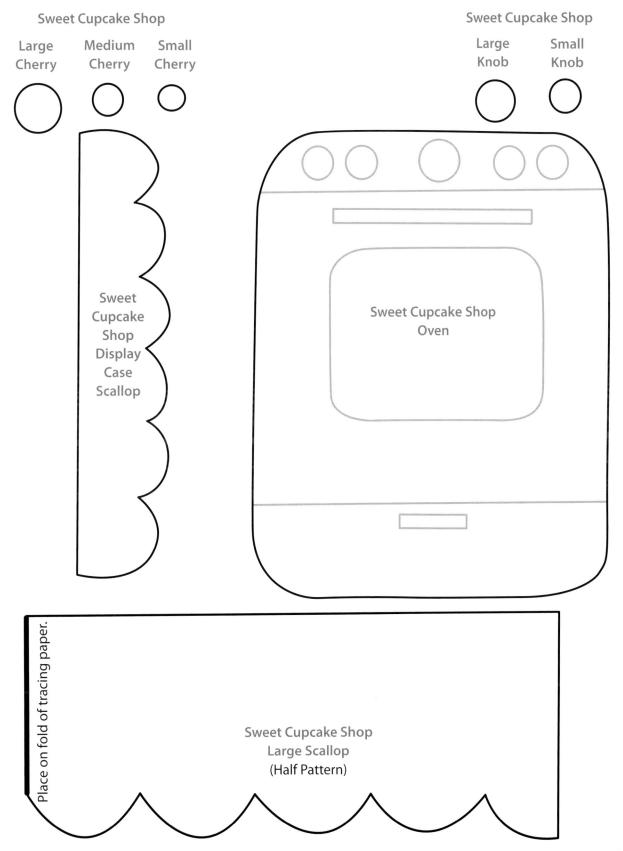

Sweet Cupcake Shop

Large Cherry

Medium Cherry

Small Cherry

Sweet Cupcake Shop

Large Knob

Small Knob

Sweet Cupcake Shop Display Case Scallop

Sweet Cupcake Shop Oven

Place on fold of tracing paper.

Sweet Cupcake Shop
Large Scallop
(Half Pattern)

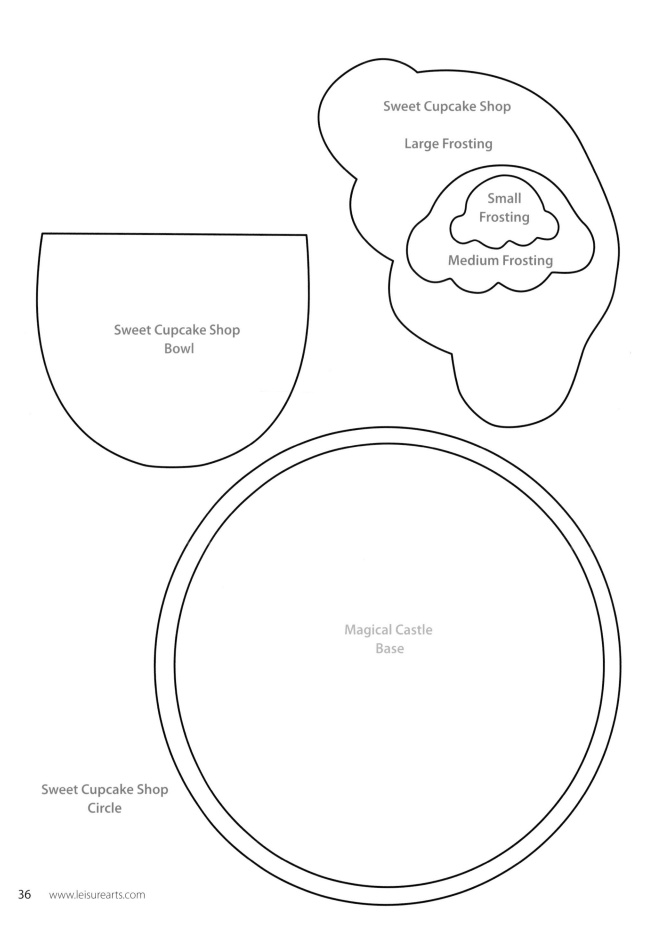

Sweet Cupcake Shop

Large Frosting

Small
Frosting

Medium Frosting

Sweet Cupcake Shop
Bowl

Magical Castle
Base

Sweet Cupcake Shop
Circle

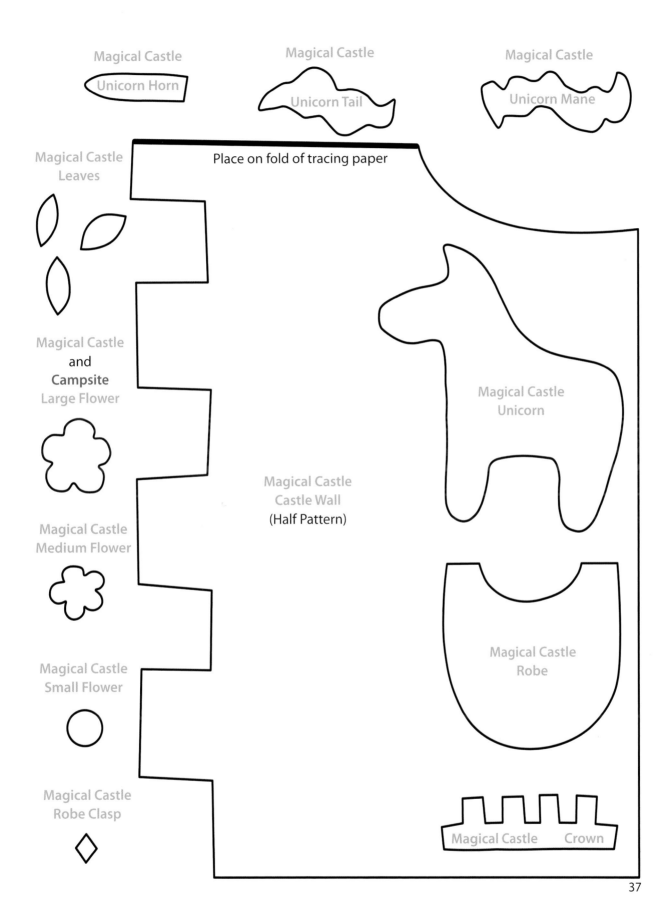

Magical Castle
Unicorn Horn

Magical Castle
Unicorn Tail

Magical Castle
Unicorn Mane

Magical Castle
Leaves

Place on fold of tracing paper

Magical Castle
and
Campsite
Large Flower

Magical Castle
Medium Flower

Magical Castle
Small Flower

Magical Castle
Robe Clasp

Magical Castle
Castle Wall
(Half Pattern)

Magical Castle
Unicorn

Magical Castle
Robe

Magical Castle   Crown

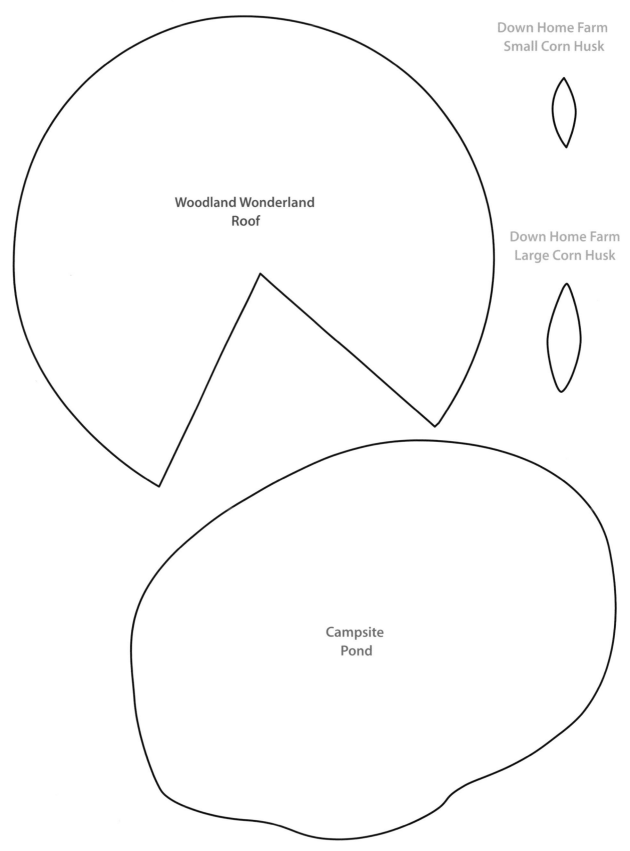

Down Home Farm
Small Corn Husk

Woodland Wonderland
Roof

Down Home Farm
Large Corn Husk

Campsite
Pond

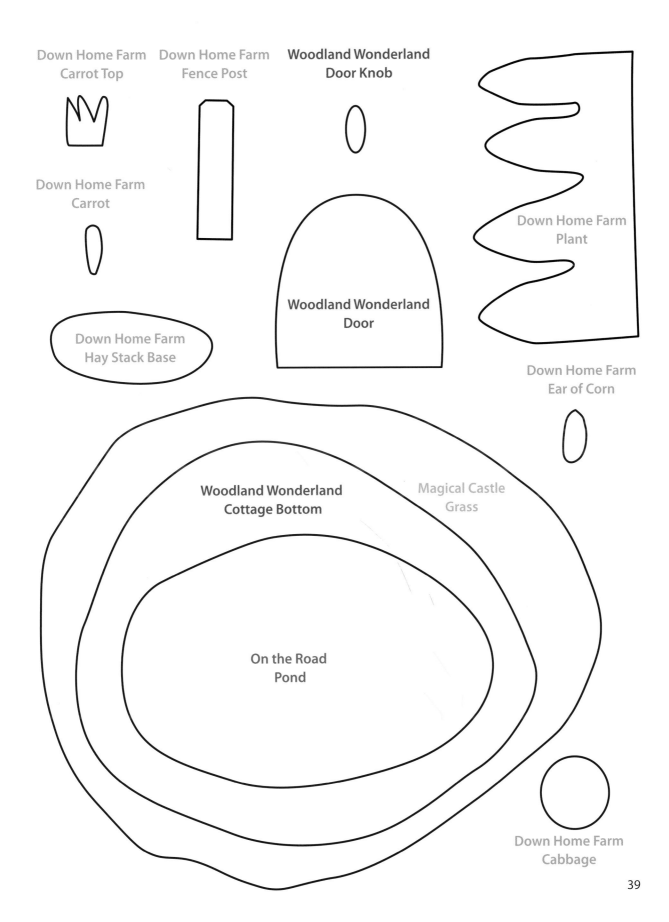

Down Home Farm
Carrot Top

Down Home Farm
Fence Post

**Woodland Wonderland
Door Knob**

Down Home Farm
Carrot

**Woodland Wonderland
Door**

Down Home Farm
Plant

Down Home Farm
Hay Stack Base

Down Home Farm
Ear of Corn

**Woodland Wonderland
Cottage Bottom**

Magical Castle
Grass

On the Road
Pond

Down Home Farm
Cabbage

39

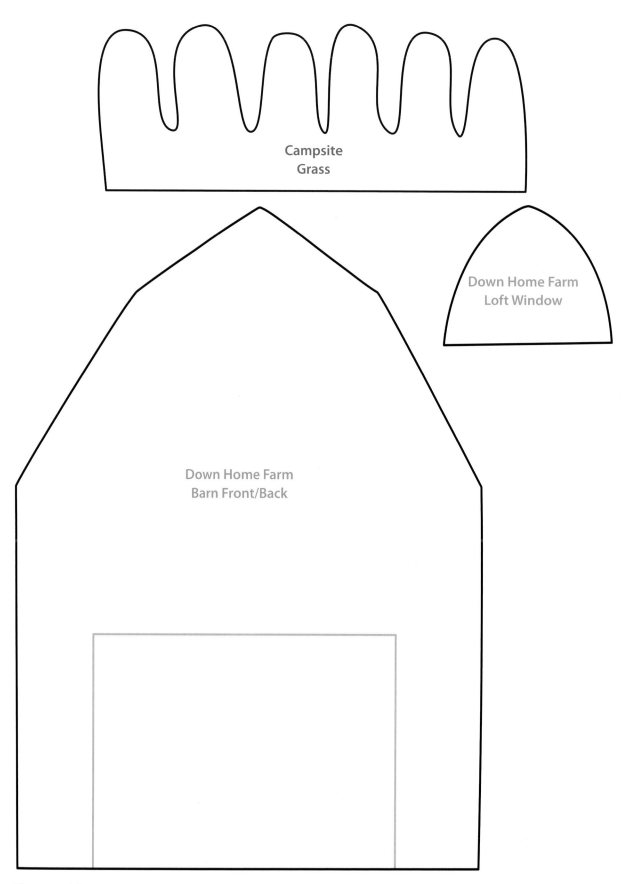

Campsite
Grass

Down Home Farm
Loft Window

Down Home Farm
Barn Front/Back

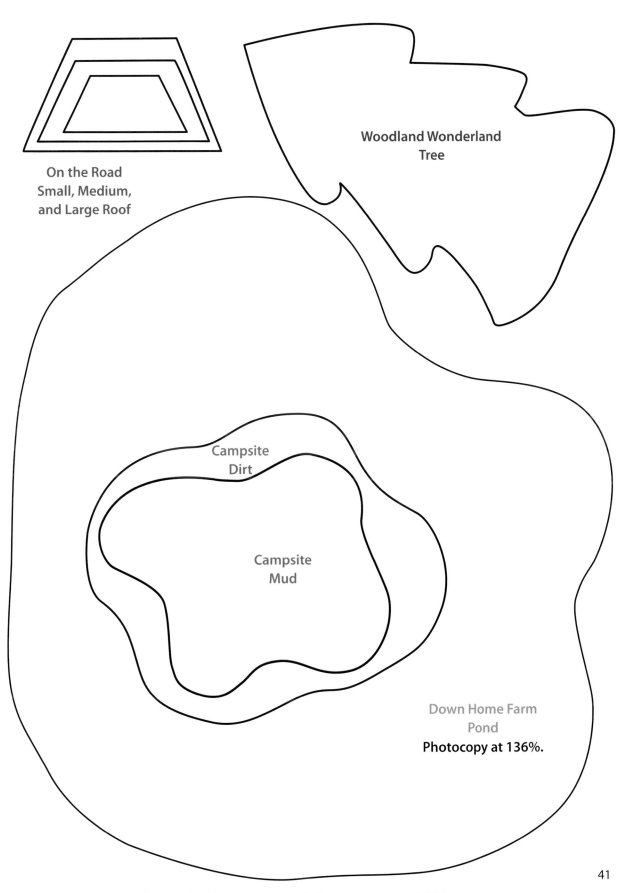

On the Road
Small, Medium,
and Large Roof

Woodland Wonderland
Tree

Campsite
Dirt

Campsite
Mud

Down Home Farm
Pond

Photocopy at 136%.

41

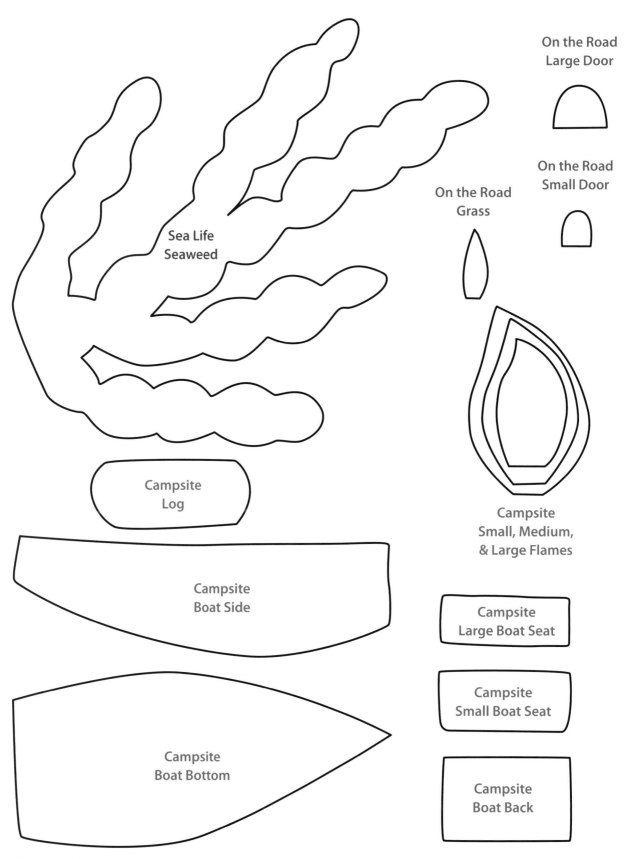

Sea Life
Seaweed

On the Road
Large Door

On the Road
Small Door

On the Road
Grass

Campsite
Log

Campsite
Small, Medium,
& Large Flames

Campsite
Boat Side

Campsite
Large Boat Seat

Campsite
Small Boat Seat

Campsite
Boat Bottom

Campsite
Boat Back

Woodland Wonderland
Hedgehog Body

Woodland Wonderland
Hedgehog Nose

On the Road
Maple Tree Top

Woodland Wonderland
Hedgehog Spines

Woodland Wonderland
Squirrel

Woodland Wonderland
Pansy

On the Road
Maple Tree Trunk

On the Road
Road

On the Road
Oak Tree Top

On the Road
Oak Tree Trunk

Sea
Life
Mast

43

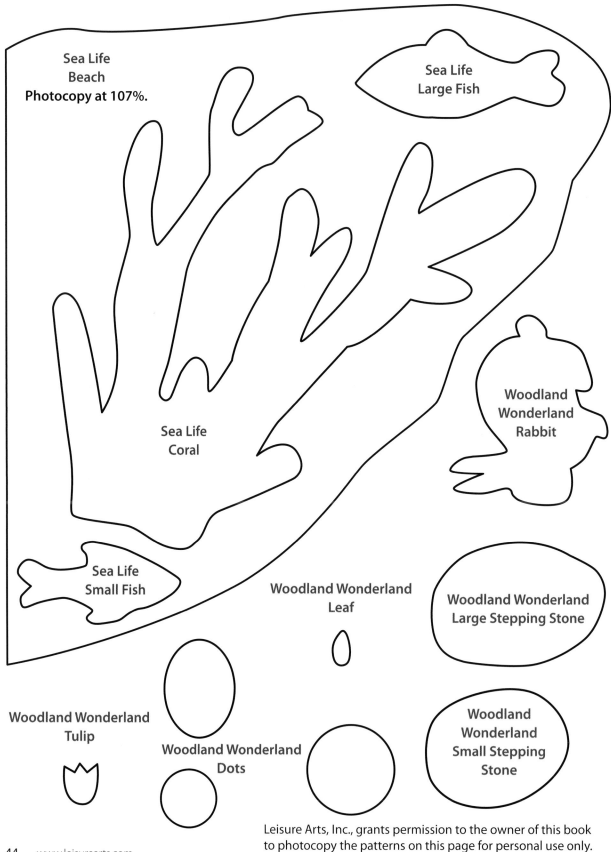

Sea Life
Beach
Photocopy at 107%.

Sea Life
Large Fish

Woodland
Wonderland
Rabbit

Sea Life
Coral

Sea Life
Small Fish

Woodland Wonderland
Leaf

Woodland Wonderland
Large Stepping Stone

Woodland Wonderland
Tulip

Woodland Wonderland
Dots

Woodland
Wonderland
Small Stepping
Stone

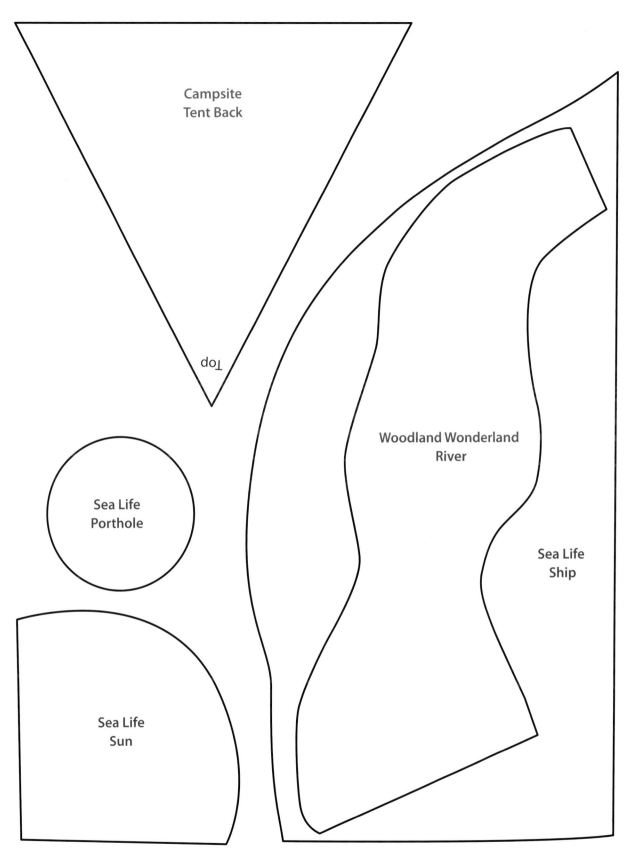

Campsite
Tent Back

Top

Sea Life
Porthole

Woodland Wonderland
River

Sea Life
Ship

Sea Life
Sun

45

General Instructions

To make your crafting easier and more enjoyable, we encourage you to carefully read all of the General Instructions and familiarize yourself with the individual project instructions before you get started.

Supplies

Supplies listed below are needed for all projects. Individual project instructions include supplies specific to that project.

FELT

Projects were made using wool felt or eco-felt. Eco-felt is made using Eco-fil™, a polyester fiber created from 100% post-consumer recycled plastic bottles. Both wool felt and eco-felt are available in approximately 9" x 12" sheets or by the yard in 36", 60", or 72" widths. Press felt using a pressing cloth.

THREAD

Projects were stitched using six-strand cotton embroidery floss. Individual project instructions specify the number of strands to use.

NEEDLES

A sharp point is necessary to pierce felt, but the size and type of needle is an individual choice. The eye needs to be large enough to accommodate the number of strands of floss you will be using.

Embroidery needles, sometimes referred to as crewel needles, usually work well. Sizes range from #3 - #10 and they are available in individual and multi-size packages. Keep in mind that the lower the number, the larger the needle.

SCISSORS

Use fabric scissors to cut out felt shapes and utility scissors for cutting paper patterns. Small sharp embroidery scissors are handy for clipping thread and trimming "fuzzies" from the edges of finished shapes.

USING PATTERNS

Trace pattern, including gray lines, onto tracing paper; cut out pattern on outer traced line.

To make a complete pattern from a half pattern, fold tracing paper in half. Place fold of tracing paper on fold line. Trace pattern; cut out. Unfold for complete pattern.

Some patterns in this book may need to be enlarged. The percentage to enlarge the pattern is stated on the pattern. Photocopy the pattern, enlarging as directed. Cut out pattern on outer line.

WORKING WITH FELT

Place patterns, traced or printed side up, on felt; pin. Cut out shapes even with edges of pattern. Repeat for each pattern piece needed for your project.

Felt does not have a right or wrong side. If a felt shape is embroidered, the stitched side becomes the right side. When instructed to layer shapes, place an embroidered shape right side up on top of another shape. For shapes that are not embroidered, simply layer the shapes.

EMBROIDERY STITCHES

Backstitch
Come up at 1, go down, at 2, and come up at 3 (**Fig. 1**). Length of stitches may be varied as desired.

Cross Stitch
Come up at 1 and go down, at 2. Come up at 3 and go down at 4 (**Fig. 2**).

Running Stitch
The running stitch consists of a series of straight stitches with the stitch length equal to the space between stitches. Come up at 1 and go down at 2. Come up at 3 and go down at 4 (**Fig. 3**).

Straight Stitch
Come up at 1 and go down at 2 (**Fig. 4**). Length of stitches may be varied as desired.

Whipstitch
Come up at 1. Go down at 2, directly across from 1 (**Fig. 5**). Come up at 3, approximately $1/16$" away from 1. Continue working in the same manner.

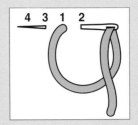

Fig. 1

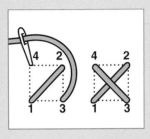

Fig. 2

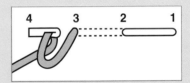

Fig. 3

Fig. 4

Fig. 5

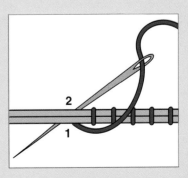

Meet Kimberly Layton

Driven by a lifelong love of making things, Kimberly Layton took her crafting to a whole new level in 2008. She is now a full-time professional blogger, craft book author, and creative business coach.

Kimberly blogs about Etsy business and all manner of DIY crafty things at EverythingEtsy.com, shares tutorials and inspiring creative ideas at HandmadeandCraft.com, and reveals her personal side at KimberlyLayton.com. She also can be found as @EverythingEtsy on Twitter, Facebook, Instagram, and Pinterest.

"I like dabbling in all kinds of crafts, but felt is my favorite," she says. Her blogging "all started with trying to promote my felt crafts that I sold in my Etsy shop. From there it grew to coaching and social media training for handmade businesses." Traveling is Kimberly's other favorite pastime. "We've visited all the states in the lower 48 and have traveled with our children as far away as the Great Barrier Reef! Just mention the word 'go' and we are there!"

Production Team: Technical Writer – Lisa Lancaster; Technical Associate – Mary Sullivan Hutcheson; Editorial Writer – Susan Frantz Wiles; Senior Graphic Artist – Lora Puls; Graphic Artist – Kellie McAnulty; Photostylists – Stephanie Moore and Lori Wenger; Photographer – Jason Masters.

Made In U.S.A.